Only Women Can Save the World

Ronald Carter

PAGE PUBLISHING, INC.
New York, NY

First originally published by Page Publishing, Inc. 2019

ISBN 978-1-64462-902-4 (Paperback)
ISBN 978-1-64462-903-1 (Digital)

Printed in the United States of America

Only women can save the world. And why is this?

Let's look at history. Everything we know about history has been told from the white man's point of view; everything in life has been presented from the white man's perspective. You, as a white woman, have to accept some of the responsibility for what has happened and is happening in the world, because white women create white men. If you create something, you have the obligation—the *right*—to instruct and to lead forward, because you are as good as your floor plan. Raising children is a very, very difficult job, but you, as the white woman, abandon that responsibility. Is it because you have resources, and having them, you feel you should have a nanny and make a priority of your appearance? In reality, I think this has led to a lack of parenting in America. Yes, parenting is gone—and in America, today's kids are out of control.

Let me talk about my mother. First of all, my mother was Lord God to me. She was *over* God, because she was *present*. I loved, honored, and obeyed her every command. My mother, a single woman, raised three boys—a woman from North Carolina who came to New York—tried three times to have a girl and had three sons. My father was a sailor, who, throughout my childhood, would pop up and spend two to three days with us and then would leave again; the next time I would see him would be four or five months later, when he would show up with no money and yet again my mother would take care of him for days and then he would be gone. For twenty years this would happen. I used to think that my father was a bad man. As I got older, I realized my father knew my mother was too strong to be controlled. Yes, my mother took no mess from no man, woman, or child!

I grew up in the South Bronx. Every kid on my block was scared of my mother!

"Your mother, she's crazy!" they'd say. You don't have to tell me that—I live with this woman! I was never absent, never late my entire school career. There were times I woke up saying "Ma, I don't want to go to school today,"; she'd respond with "You're going out of here or I'm going to kill your ass!" The second time she said it, I was wide awake—no longer feeling sick—and I got ready for school. My mother showed no mercy and gave no breaks. You did what you were told to do without question. My mother was like a Marine drill sergeant at the table: "You sit here, *you* sit here, and you sit *here.*" Those were your seats; you never sat in another seat, only the one she told you to. You set your clothes out the night before so that in the morning you had ten minutes in the bathroom to get dressed and leave for school on time, *all* the time.

My mother never negotiated. She would say, "Go to the store, bring my change and a receipt, and the change better be right."

One time I didn't count the change.

"Come here, boy, and count this change."

"Mom, it's a penny! We're on the fifth floor, and it's raining—hard!"

"Take all that stuff back, and go get my money before I kill your ass!"

I counted the change every time thereafter.

Yes, my mother was no joke. I didn't get many beatings, but the ones I got served a purpose. One comes to mind: Back in 1968, everybody had a key chain. One day I found a key chain, threw the keys away, and kept the chain.

"Mom," I pleaded, "I want keys to the house."

She replied, "You don't need no keys, I'm home, I don't work. All you want is to be like the other kids. Okay, I'm going to give you keys. If you lose them, I'm going to kill your ass!"

Well, I had the keys for three weeks; then one day I was playing on the swing, not paying attention, and the yard was almost empty. I jumped out of the swing and ran so that I wouldn't be late for lunch. I could never explain to my mother about being late, and the keys must have fallen off my neck. I got to class and told the teacher, "Oh, I've got to go to the bathroom!" I ran back up to the swings, but I could not find the keys. So at three o'clock, I wrote my mother a letter:

> *Mom, I lost the keys, and I'm not ready to die, so I'm not coming home.*

I gave the letter to my younger brother and went to the after-school center, thinking, "What am I going to do at five o'clock when this place closes?"

My brother came to get me. "Mom said she's not going to kill you," he said. "You can come home."

"What?" I thought. "This woman don't give no breaks!"

Finally I got to the door. I listened to make sure the commercials were off and her stories were on. I walked right by her, and she said nothing; I thought I was safe.

"You take off your school clothes and put on play clothes," she hollered as soon she heard the zipper of my pants. "Did I not tell you I'm going to kill you if you lost those keys?"

And she kicked my ass! I haven't lost anything since then, and that was fifty years ago. You don't understand it when it happens, but you understand it later on: Strong parenting is necessary, as we can see today, when kids with guns are killing kids and other kids are killing parents. How can this be?

Here it is, in 2018, and white women—*all* women—are treated with less respect than they deserve. No man has given life to another man, nor to woman, and yet women do every day. Women are the superior beings! When God made women, she gave them the "life box." The life box is where life comes from! There are two types of life boxes: there is the *supremely* good life box (that's a box that nothing has come out of), and then there is the extremely good life box (from which a male or a female child has come out). The box should have a warning label! The power of the box is incredible; the life box is the most sought-after thing on this planet. We all know someone who has done something crazy because of that life box. In reality, size does not matter; if you witness a body—a whole body—coming out of that life box, no matter how much you jump up and down, no matter how big your wiener is, there is nothing you can do with it.

For some reason, the white man has in inferiority complex when it comes to his penis. Growing up, I used to have a white phobia;

both of my brothers were darker than me, both had bigger wieners, and I had a sixth finger. So I was the "white" child, and until I was eleven years old, I was forced to deal with that, I thought being white was a good thing; once I was able to read up on the things that the white man had done, I no longer wanted to be white. So I picked at my sixth finger until I needed surgery to have it removed. Once my finger was removed, I was no longer "white."

Here it is today, fifty years later, and the white man is still doing terrible things to people. When will it end? When will they conquer their inferiority complexes?

You, as a white woman, have to accept some of the blame for this. White women create white men. You are the creator, and yet you abandon your responsibility to guide, to direct, and to instruct them on the good things which they should do. Case in point: Charles Manson's mother abandoned him at age nine, and look at the monster he turned out to be!

Yes, women, it's time. It's time for all women—not just white women, but *all* women—to step up and save the world we live in. If we continue to leave control of the world in the white man's hands, we are destined to be destroyed. White women you have the ear of the white man; the white man is your partner, he is your husband, and he is your companion. This is the white man's system, and this is the white man's society.

Remember, it's a woman's world now; men just run it, and to get this done women have to step up to save us! For one thing, you have to give him the top item on his bucket list. What's that? That's experiencing three women at one time. Yes, give him the ultimate physical experience! In return, he has to agree to three conditions:

Number one, if there's a prenuptial agreement, it has to be destroyed. Here it is, women: the white man's priority list. Number one is his money, then it's his wiener, then it's his guns or his car, *then* you as the woman. The second thing you have to do is get the guns. Some white men feel that the more guns they have, the stronger they are. The third thing—the most important thing—is that he has to train you to be his replacement, because it's a woman's world now! Men only run it, and we have to get the right women in position to save the world.

I know I'm not the only man who loved, honored, and obeyed every command his mother issued. I'm sure there is nothing greater than the mother; she is the creator. I was in fear of my mother for fourteen years. She had total control; no nonsense, no play, never forgiving. You obeyed her every command. Today, I'm so glad that I was trained properly by her, because it made me a better person.

The things that the white man is doing today are incredible, and what's worse is that they are denying them—saying that they aren't happening, that they aren't doing them, taking no account-ability for their actions, especially against women. We are subject to being destroyed if we continue to allow this to happen!

Yes, women, let's look at history. We have the Founding Fathers, honored in memorials and museums; yet every one of them was white, and therefore every one of them was given life by a white woman. We have Mount Rushmore; what's that? Five men, no women—white men created by white women. Where is the mountain monument for women? Today, the white man continues to try to brainwash women into thinking they are inferior and subordinate.

When women give the white man's life—and here it is women create men—there will be no more prejudices, because all women have the life box. All women have the potential to give life, whether they have blonde hair or blue hair, whether they are fat or skinny, whether they are short or tall. They possess the most sought-after thing in the world: they can give life. Men, knowing this, have tried to brainwash women into being subordinate.

As I've said, my mother was the Lord God to me—in fact, she was more than God, because I always knew she was there. You talk to God and hope for a response; my mother *commanded* and had total control. Yes, women, you too have to step forward and begin the process of taking over! We have women in the military and in the police department; when women gain total control, they should form a committee and go to every precinct and get these scared white boys out! Too many times, we seen an unarmed black man shot by a scared white policeman. The cop has a gun; the black man had nothing. How could you be in fear of your life when *you* had the only weapon? We have seen this happen so many times all over the world; Chicago, a seventeen-year-old child was shot sixteen times by a police officer—a man, not a woman. Ninety percent of the police force may be good. but it's that crooked 10% we have to get out of there! Here in the Bronx, we saw a video of a young black kid running into his house and locking himself in the bathroom; a white cop follows him into the house and kills the child. How could this happen? What could the child have done? He had no weapon, and still he was killed.

White women, when you do take over, the most important thing that you have to do is enact the Bobbitt Law. This law will state that if you rape a woman, or if you do any physical harm to a woman, you can be publicly castrated. That's right—just like the way white men did in the past, lynching black men and cutting their penises off. If white men could be subject to the same horrible fate for violating a woman in a woman's world, it would totally eliminate rape. In countries where you steal and the courts sentence you to have your hand cut off, there is very little stealing because someone would see you and know what you've done.

The white man shows no love towards other white men; the white man shows no love to anyone. Today, we have rich white men telling workers that the problem is black and brown people, who are working just like them, trying to survive. We are living in the white man's system and the white man's society, and as we know, all white men are created by white women. Look at the white man's perspective: In the 1600s, there was no such thing as the "white race." This was constructed in the colonial. Of time to sustain white supremacy. Before that, if you were from England, you were English; if you were from Scotland, you were Scottish; if you were from Germany, you were German; and if you were from Ireland, you were Irish. But in the colonial era, to get all these nationalities on the same team—the "white race"—you had to brainwash people into believing that they are better because they are "white," not black, and therefore not a slave. A nation was created based on the idea that being white is superior, and yet its founders said "We hold these truths to be self-evident: that *all men* are created equal." This is a lie!

Now, the white mentality has further developed the idea that being white is better, and today the white man—created by the white woman—is using this ideology to perpetuate racism. It is 2018, and white supremacy is at its peak. Consider: people do not choose the President. You *want* the people to choose the person they want to run for President, to continue the illusion that America is a democracy; but when you pledge allegiance, that allegiance is to "the Republic for which it stands." So why is America called a democracy? The word *democracy* is not in the Preamble; the word *democracy* is not in the Constitution; the word *democracy* is not in the Constitution of any of the fifty states. So remember, for this reason, America is a republic, not a democracy.

Written in 1865, the Thirteenth Amendment to the Constitution states you are free. Then you have the Fourteenth Amendment, which was created in 1866 and states that you are granted equal protection under the law. But the Fourteenth Amendment wasn't ratified until 1868! So what were you between 1865 and 1868? You were a "resident," and you are still a resident today. We confuse the words *liberty* and *freedom*; white people have freedom, and black people have liberty. Freedom is the ability to make decisions without external control, whereas liberty is the ability to make decisions *because* of external control. Because of this, the white man still owns you! Abraham Lincoln emancipated the slaves, which means to let someone go from bondage, but it also means transferring ownership from the individual to the state. These things have been done by the white man, who was given life by the white woman—and without her consent, because the white man has total control! This must end.

We need women to step up and become Lord God's like my mother to be the leaders in which man needs. I'll give you an example. There are so many great women in this world who will never be recognized for their greatness, like one woman who is Lord God to her seven children in New York—five girls and two boys. She is so great she took on a foster child, another boy. But she was still not done! She took on *another* foster child that was white; through the process of adopting this white child, the people at the agency assessed her. Do you think it will be a problem with your children? Do you think it would be a problem in the neighborhood she lived in was Harlem? Do you think it was a problem because the child is white? Her response was simple: "There will be no problem."

I didn't even know then he was white! I just thought he was light-skinned. This is the woman known to me as Mother, and known to the child as the Lord God. I love this woman and I always will. How good is this woman? Simply amazing! Just to be willing to take on two more children after having seven in New York shows the power which women possess. After my mother's passing, a woman came into my life; a woman with six daughters in New York, one mentally challenged, and all with different fathers—and she still maintained her sanity! My wife's mother had five daughters and one son; she's also a God. She took on two foster children. How can these women do this in a man's world?

If you are a white woman with resources, your first step should not be getting a nanny. Hiring a nanny means abandoning your responsibility to raise, to guide, and to dictate proper behavior to your creation. This is what creates monsters! Where's the bond between a rapist and his mother? Your mother represents your first model of a woman. She shows you what you should think of women, and there is nothing greater than a mother; and yet some white women choose to make their priority looking good and being well-dressed for their man. They want to be a trophy wife for their husband, but in the white man's mind the priority is his money, then his penis, then his guns or his car. That's what women should realize that women have to step forward!

I don't know why we are living in a period of time in which the white man's inferiority complex and white entitlement are at their peak. When will the white man ever accept what they themselves have stated: that "we hold these truths to be self-evident, that all men are created equal"? Of course, this is not true; but it should be!

My college experience was amazing. I left New York on August 31, 1975, at noon. I was supposed to be at Wheeling College in Wheeling, West Virginia, by noon for freshman orientation, but at the time my girlfriend was having my first son, and my mother did not want me to go to college thinking I was going to abandon my responsibility to take care of my son. Nonetheless, I was determined to experience college. Up until that time, I had been selling drugs and running numbers. I wanted to have a real life, not one of illegal activities, so I stayed up all night until my mother went to sleep to take $32 from her wallet so I could pay for my ticket.

I grew up in the South Bronx. I was the first child on my block to go to college. So here I was, in Pittsburgh, Pennsylvania, and the bus driver made the announcement: "Wheeling, West Virginia, next stop!" And that's when it hit me: I'd never left New York before! I had seven dollars and a trunk with some clothes, which I had taken out of the closet at the last minute. I didn't know where the school was; I didn't know where the bus station was—I knew absolutely nothing. It was midnight, so I had to ask *somebody*. I looked around the bus and there was one man who wasn't asleep, so I went to him and I said, "Sir, by chance, do you know where Wheeling College is?"

He looked at me and said "Yes, I do—I worked there."

"Thank you, sir," I said, and I went back to my seat—and a white halo came over me. That's right: a white halo—and from that moment on, since August 31, 1975, I have never doubted, or even considered, that anything and everything would work out for the best for me. I'm good at the game of life, and life is good to me!

When the bus stopped, he got off and I got off; he went to the phone and called Mr. Paul Baker, who happened to be the basketball coach at Wheeling College. He happened to be the individual that I talked to at a seminar that was given at my high school in the Bronx, Christopher Columbus High. In ten minutes, Coach Baker picked us up, transported us to the school. I was in a room with my name on the door!

The other resident of my dorm room, when he found out that I was black, transferred out of the school. This was a school with a student body of 450 whites and eleven blacks; they brought in eighteen more black students that year, and thirteen transferred by December. I was fascinated, because in my mind, whites hated blacks but didn't have animosity toward one another. Boy, was I wrong! My college experience showed me white supremacy on a high level.

The first two people I talked to at the school were Asian. Never before had I seen identical twins. I asked one of them, "If you were to dig in your right ear, would your brother have a sensation and dig in his left ear?" They looked at one another, and then he said, "I'm Japanese. He's Korean." To hell with him! I couldn't believe it. They looked alike and were wearing the same clothes. That was my introduction to racism. Unbelievable! Dominicans, Puerto Ricans, Jews, Germans…do you want some black racism? One brother told me I was a slave and he never was, because he paid for his ticket to come from Africa!

I'll tell you one thing that happened at college that really, really disturbed me. I grew up with an inferiority complex; I was considered to be "white" by my brothers. They had bigger wieners, I was lighter-skinned than they were, and I had a sixth finger on one hand. I went from practically being a Martian to being "white" because my mother never said anything about it. I accepted it until I was at college. On a few occasions, I would be in a room with six or seven other guys, and the conversation would be about baseball, basketball, football, or girls. Out of the clear blue sky, a white boy would start talking about his penis, saying "seven and a half inches," "eight and a half inches," and so on. I would become livid! I found that to be very, very insulting. Why would you say that to impress another man? The white boys would tell me they wanted me to think that they weren't a "normal" white man with a little wiener. Who cares?

Women have to help white men get over their inferiority complex about their wieners. I'm a man with a small wiener, but I do not feel inferior to any man. Growing up, I was taught lovemaking by a lesbian couple who showed me how to take grapes, hold them with my teeth, and use my tongue to spin them around and around. They also showed me toy play. In the '70s I was using toys on girls, giving them ultimate pleasure—to the point that they told their mothers, and I got to experience mothers and daughters, because their husbands and their fathers didn't believe in toy play!

Today, the life box is still the most sought-after thing on the planet. If you, as a man, want to evaluate your wiener, procreate. Create a man! Create a woman! This will show you if your wiener is good or not, because size does not matter. If you witness a whole body coming out of that life box, you know no matter what size your wiener, no matter how much you jump up and down in that box, there is nothing you can do to it.

I'll give you a case in point. My best friend is a brother who's a football player. He is 6'4 and weighs about 260 pounds; his wife is 5'3 and weighs about 130 pounds. She gave birth to a set of twins, each weighing 8 pounds 4 ounces. He was in the delivery room when he saw those babies coming out of that box; he said he dropped to his knees and cried. They didn't know who was crying more, the two babies or him! He told me it took him nine months to have sex with his wife again after witnessing two bodies coming out of that box.

Women, only you can give life in that manner! This is why you fail to accept your superiority. No man can do that, and this is why in white society, the white man continues to try to brainwash you, as a woman, that you are inferior. How could this be? Women, it's time! There should be a sense of the importance of women stepping forward to save the world. Look at the state of the world: We have children killing other children. This is because of guns. In Florida, a couple takes in a child and believes it's okay for him to have a gun in their house; so it's not a matter of if, it's a matter of when and where. Kids today are so out of control from the lack of parenting!

My mother, if she was alive today, would be in jail. She never, ever had any child curse around her. I grew up on a street in the South Bronx, and every kid on that block was scared of my mother. "Yo, your mother was crazy!" they'd say. You don't have to tell me that—I've lived with this woman all my life!

The summer of 1967 comes to mind: This kid, a redhead named David, broke a bottle and cut his mother on the arm because she wouldn't buy him ice cream. My mother was downstairs, and here comes this boy, who knew me. "How you doing, Ms. Carter?" he said.

"Son, let me tell you something," she replied. "Your mother, she's a better woman than me. Because if you would've cut *me*, I would've killed your ass! You'd be dead right now." My mother got all close to him, and I was so glad that he just stood there and cried, because if he would've sucked his teeth or said something stupid like "Mind your business," my mother would've choked him.

Let's say you were getting a beating for doing something wrong, and you raised your hand to catch the belt. "What, you trying to hit *me*?" she'd say, and she would throw the belt away and choke you. So when you got a beating, you *took* your beating. I have friends whose mother used to beat them with sticks. That's parenting at its best! That's old school!

There are so many great women in this world, and women have to come together. You are the majority, and the system is set up where the majority rules—but still we see that the white man will manipulate things to his advantage. Look at this past election; the outcome was the fault of women. Yes, women! You blew it! A woman had the chance to be the President of the United States. If every woman that voted pulled the lever for Hillary Clinton, she would have won by a landslide. But you women did not look at the big picture. The white man that's in the White House has no love for women; you heard the tapes—he is a man who insults women. I had a woman tell me "You think I should vote for Hillary just because I got a pussy." Why, certainly! That's the most powerful thing on the planet. How can you have a negative view of Hillary with all that she's accomplished? All that she achieved was done in a man's world in which she was at disadvantage, as all women are. She would've made a great president.

Women have been presidents in other countries, but it has to happen in America for it to mean something here. Recently, it came out that women will be allowed to drive in Saudi Arabia! American women have so many advantages; the white woman has every advantage there is. I thought there would be a woman president before a black man, and yet we had Barack Obama for eight years—and now we have a white man, a *rich* white man, who shows no love to anyone who is not rich or white. Women, remember: the white woman had three million—that's right, *three million*—more votes, and the white man's manipulation led to the white man becoming president.

This is another reason for women to step up, not just to save the system, but to save the world. I hope it happens. I know it should, but only time will tell. I love women; I always will my mother was the greatest woman I've ever known. I just hope and pray that one-day woman will be in control!

I guess maybe this will happen and if it does happen may be women will form a three women panel of panel that will have a high ranking military woman a high ranking police woman and a woman Doctor.

Women, once they gain control, should form a three-woman president panel; one woman will have the ear of the Democratic Party, one woman will have the ear of the Republican Party, and they will form a new party—the People's party—this party will be for all people, rich, poor, and foreign. And they will decide if together the three-woman president panel should consist with a woman from the military, a woman from the police department, and a woman doctor. I also would like to suggest that when women gain control they think about forming a new race a race where you are either Brown or you are Beige the letter B is the same you would be looked upon as being the same whether you are Brown or you are beige looked at as being a male or a female or not sure and you would be judged as being the same. When this day come women I hope will be fair to everyone we must in this hatred in America today women can do this women must do this God no she gave the ability to give life to women and she wants women to save life

My mother was Lord God to me and all mothers should be looked at as being Lord God.

About the Author

Ronald Carter was born in New York, raised in the South Bronx, and went to college in West Virginia. He loves women and respects them greatly. His mother was his god

www.ingramcontent.com/pod-product-compliance
Lightning Source LLC
Chambersburg PA
CBHW051429250726
48655CB00003B/1323